Really WILD

WHALES

Claire Robinson

First published in Great Britain by Heinemann Library,
Halley Court, Jordan Hill, Oxford OX2 8EJ,
a division of Reed Educational and Professional Publishing Ltd.

Heinemann is a registered trademark of Reed Educational & Professional Publishing Limited.

OXFORD MELBOURNE AUCKLAND
JOHANNESBURG BLANTYRE GABORONE
IBADAN PORTSMOUTH NH (USA) CHICAGO

Designed by Celia Floyd
Illustrations by Alan Fraser (Pennant Illustration)
Printed and bound in Hong Kong/China by South China Printing Co.

03 02 01 00 99
10 9 8 7 6 5 4 3 2 1

ISBN 0 431 02874 5

British Library Cataloguing in Publication Data

Robinson, Claire
Whale. – (Really wild)
1. Whales – Juvenile literature
I. Title
599.5

Look at the whale at the bottom of each page. Flick the pages and see what happens!

Acknowledgements
The Publishers would like to thank the following for permission to reproduce photographs:
Ardea London Ltd: Francois Gohier, pp.4 (left and right), p.9, 11, 12-13, 18, 20, 22, Mike Osmond p.7, Jean-Paul Ferrero p.14, J.M La Roque p.17; Bruce Coleman: Mr Johnny Johnson p.15; Natural History Unit: Doc White pp.8, 16, 19, 23; Oxford Scientific Films: Zig Leszczynski p.5 (left), Mark Newman p.5 (right), Ben Osborne p.6, C.J. Gilbert p.10, Duncan Murrell p.21.

Cover photograph: Ardea/Francois Gohier.

Contents

Some words are shown in bold, **like this**. You can find out what they mean by looking in the glossary.

Whale relatives

Whales are very large **mammals** that live in the sea. Instead of hair they grow a thick layer of fat, called **blubber**, to keep them warm in cold waters.

grey whale

sperm whale

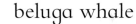
beluga whale

humpback whale

There are more than 30 different kinds of whale. Humpback whales are one of the largest. Let's see how they live.

Where do whales live?

Humpback whales are found all over the world. They spend most of the year in the icy cold seas around the **Arctic** and **Antarctic**.

Before winter arrives they **migrate** to warmer parts of the world to **mate** and give birth.

Diving and breathing

Whales swim by moving their tails up and down. Long flippers help them turn and dive. They can stay underwater for half an hour between breaths.

This whale has come to the surface to breathe air. When whales breathe out through their **blowholes**, water on top of their head is blown upwards.

Finding food

The cold seas are filled with good food. The whales eat lots of tiny animals called **krill**. Krill look like small shrimps.

The whale shoots upwards in the water with its mouth wide open. Its throat stretches wider as it fills up with krill.

Eating

Look at the **baleen** inside this whale's mouth. It is like a sieve and traps the **krill** inside, but lets the water out.

These whales are feeding together. They trap the krill by blowing a bubble net. The whales swim inside the ring of bubbles to eat the krill.

Migrating

As winter draws near, the humpback whales **migrate** in groups to warmer seas hundreds of miles away. They go there to **mate**.

Humpbacks like to swim near the **coast**. Sometimes they poke their heads above the surface to look around. Can you see this whale's eye?

Babies

Now the male sings strange and beautiful songs. He hopes the females will hear and come to **mate**. After mating it will be 11 months before a baby is born.

A humpback whale gives birth to one **calf**. This calf is one week old. As soon as he was born, his mother pushed him to the surface to breathe.

Growing up

The whale **calf** stays close to his mother. In spring, they **migrate** back to the cold seas with other humpback whales.

As they grow up, whales learn how to find **krill**, and how to hold their breath as they dive. They love splashing about in the water.

Whales and people

Humpback whales are gentle giants. People have hunted them for the oil in their **blubber** and for their meat. Now there are not many left.

It is hard to believe how big they are.
Look at the size of this whale's tail!
It is as wide as a car.

Humpback whale facts

- Whales are **mammals**; they feed their babies on milk and breathe air like humans.

- You can spot a humpback whale because of its humped back and the lumps on its head.

- Humpback whales can grow up to 16 metres (46 feet) long.

- Humpback whales can live for up to 45 years.

- Humpback whales are the only whales that sing songs. The songs can be heard many kilometres away through the water.

- They have very long flippers that are white underneath and have lumpy edges.

- Humpback whales have no teeth. Instead, they sieve their food through 350 layers of **baleen**.

Glossary

Arctic   the cold, northern tip of the world
Antarctic   the cold, southern tip of the world
baleen   a fringe of stiff layers that acts as a sieve
blowhole   nostrils on top of a whale's head
blubber   fat on a whale's body
calf   a baby whale
coast   land near the sea
krill   tiny sea animals that look like shrimps
mammal   a warm-blooded animal that feeds its babies on milk, some mammals have hair
mate   to find or be a partner to have babies with
migrate   make a long journey every year

Index